Eye of the Witness

AF624538

Joanna Manly

BookLeaf Publishing

Presentation by *BookLeaf Publishing*

Web: www.bookleafpub.com

E-mail: info@bookleafpub.com

ISBN: 978-93-95784-88-7

First edition 2022

To my family and friends, thank you for never giving up on me and my many interests.

ACKNOWLEDGEMENT

Firstly I would like to acknowledge BookLeaf Publishing, without whom this book of poetry would not be.
Secondly I would like to acknowledge my fellow poet, M. J. Farrell, who encouraged me to participate in this writing challenge.

PREFACE

This collection of poems I have written has seen many places while I have travelled, some of the poems are inspired from things I saw, some from things people said, from feelings, and yet others were from experiences I had. I hope that these poems can be an interesting place for you, my readers, to immerse yourselves.

Her

She sustains life, but is also a reaper to many,
Breathing in and out, her lifeblood is never
ending,
Each day will differ, every moment unique,
She is the gentle and caring mother, yet her
wrath is ferocious and roils like thunder,
Her never ending beauty goes on, as endless as
the stars above,
She has numerous treasures that only she knows
where they're found, where she takes them and
for how long they travel undisturbed, no one
knows,
Timeless she is, for none can attest to when she
began nor will end,
Problems are eased by just gazing at her
elegance,
She swishes across the ground as silk through
fingertips,
The infinite grace that she shows is visible to all.

21/8/22
Inspired by the ocean, and the multitude of
shells that were there.

Him

He takes life with the swish of a hand, yet he also carries and cradles,
He watches and waits to perform great feats, ever the master of performance,
He can be a trickster and loves to play, swooping past and causing panic as oft items go astray,
With a gentle soul as a father figure, yet also the temper of crashing waves,
His preference a brisk day, though he does enjoy the sting of heat,
Watching over the multitudes, waiting for his moment,
Where he goes and if he stays, we can not attest to,
His embrace is soft as butter, lovely to be encompassed within,
His breaths never ending, presence ever near,
Ongoing elegance known to all.

22/8/22
Inspired by the wind.

We

Burning with a passion so bright that none can compare,
We lift higher and higher into the sky above,
Lighting the night with our fiery gaze, we dance at dangerous speed,
The fanatic inside is let free, as with a smouldering glance we consume the ground,
Frantic in our movements as we seek to destroy, the glint of joy evident,
The ember of our delight grows into a blaze,
The power we possess is oft sought out,
We can choose to be calm, movements soft as a feather,
We prefer chaos and throw control to the wind,
The haze we incur brings a thrill, the show we put on is sure to enchant.

23/8/22
Inspired by fire.

They

Darkness, warmth and comfort they enjoy,
soothing motion and slight noise too,
The longer time passes the more cramped they get, not as pleasant anymore they move around,
Suddenly there is a squeeze and everything is squashed, a few more times the feeling repeats,
After a while they are thrust into bright light and the shock sets in, it's loud and they are forced to stand,
They panic and wish to return to the bliss, then gentle nudges and reassuring words are murmured, confusion is eased and they calm down.

24/8/22
Inspired by the thought of a calf being born.

Night

Closing in to block the sky, encasing everything with a quiet goodbye,
Slowly the colour drains, twinkles cover the domains,
A gentle breeze passes and weaves, brushing softly through the leaves.

25/8/22

Axe

Perching proud overhead, reminiscent of times gone by,
Slowly aging as the seasons pass, grains fading with the sun,
Long dull is my blade, many a year goes on,
Though old I am, of use I can be if ever the need arise.

29/8/22
Inspired by the biggest axe in Australia - in Kew, NSW.

Maiden

The maid of the sea sings her melody, soft and sweet as the sea,
She strokes her hair as the waves brush against the rock,
She has dwelt here long, in the midst of the ocean flora,
The home of the maid is covered in treasures, bright and dull alike,
Many envy the maiden's garden that is fit for a queen,
The colours are plenty and in every hue the imagination can conjure,
Listen to her song and do not look to the maiden, for watch her too long and lost you'll be in her never ending gaze.

29/8/22

Lizard

Little feet scurry over the ground,
Heart beating so fast,
Am I safe? Can I stop and rest?
Tail swishes over the ground,
Tongue tasting the air,
Did I get away? Is there somewhere to rest?
Shooting past the reaching grasps,
Rushing into a crack to dwell.

29/8/22

Inspired by seeing young children holding a small lizard.

Heat

Pressing in all around,
Causing rivers to flow,
Minds slow and thoughts slur,
Pinching close, it's strangling presence is felt,
Glistening in the air,
Shimmering along the ground,
Insistent on breaking us down.

30/8/22
Inspired by heat and sweat.

She

Stepping gingerly into a box, she looks to find her favourite spot,
Softly calling she snuggles down, balls of fluff gather 'round,
Kneading as though on a blanket,
Safe and secure in a warm embrace,
She begins to vibrate with contentment, the rumble audible to all,
She is happy as can be, looking after her babies.

30/8/22
Inspired by a cat with her kittens.

Helpful?

The twinge of guilt is ever there, hiding in the back,
I should help, I feel in the way,
It's their job, yet I feel useless,
I should help, I feel so bad,
Service is paid for, yet still I'm unsure,
I should help, I feel like a pain,
Is it good if I do things, will that just cause more work,
Should I help? Am I in the way?
Sitting still doing my thing, anxious as to what to do,
Should I help? Am I a pain?

31/8/22
Inspired by being in a hotel room when room service are working in there.

Galaxy

Vast and unending beauty spreads moment by
moment, to witness this journey is a desire
sought out,
Gorgeous emerald greens, blazing royal blues,
precious rose pinks, outstanding fiery oranges,
and every colour in between,
Elegant artistry, unable to be captured in full,
Soft and wispy nebulae aplenty, swirling and
curling milky-way,
Ever the twinkle and burn of stars, many a
planet and moon to see,
Secrets undiscovered are hidden away, waiting
for their time to shine,
Nestled among these marvels, all life will be
forever more.

1/9/22

Dinosaur

A loud roar from the distant past, shaking
thumps along the ground,
Scaly skin covered in scars, spikes long as arms,
Heart-stopping gaze would cause any to quiver,
teeth pointy and ever so sharp,
Would you venture near? I wouldn't dare.
He is a majestic creature, smart and quick.

2/9/22
Inspired by a friend commenting that a dinosaur "stokes the imagination".

Remember

Emotions and memories are changing with time,
some still cherished, yet also cause an ache,
If I could turn back time, what would I say?
The good times are clouded by the not so good,
though I still care,
If I could do it all over differently, would I?
I still think of what could have been, but I know
it wouldn't have worked,
I've moved on now, but what if I hadn't?
Wondering how you are, but knowing I can't
ask,
I haven't forgotten you, have you forgotten me?

4/9/22
Inspired by past friendships and relationships.

Hard Times

Once a community of farming, turned to tourism
for it was such a success,
Many the number that came and went, ever a
place of interest,
Thriving and full of life, then in came a plague
full of malice,
From trading all of the time, to staff having
hardly any work,
From home away from home, to a place to keep
the isolated, the changes were aplenty,
These are the hardships we have faced, but we
will conquer it once and for all, no matter how
long it takes.

4/9/22
Inspired by covid and it's effect going through
Fiji and it's hotels.

I

Sparkling in the morning light, drifting on a breeze,
Light as a feather I climb up high,
Dancing gracefully through the night, I land with a flourish,
I am a star of the show and many marvel at my beauty,
What colour am I? Can you tell? Crystalline I can appear, glimmering in the light,
Look closely for soon I shall disappear, I am unique, there is no other such as I.

4/9/22
Inspired by a snowflake.

Underwater

Close your eyes and listen to the magical
silence,
Enjoy the brief tranquillity while it lasts,
Breathe and hear the muffled sounds through the
water,
In this space you are safe and light as a feather,
Feel the ripples lap against your body,
Time means nothing here, enjoy it in full,
Slow your heart and trust yourself,
This moment will be locked in eternity.

7/9/22
Inspired by floating in a pool.

Wonderland

Mountains and valleys stretching on, clumps of amazing coloured vegetation,
Gliding above and watching it all pass underneath, marvelling at all there is to see,
The multitude of life passing by, some coming close to say hello, others rushing by and off to hide,
The incredible variety of hues are spread wide for one to view,
Take the chance to dive into the wonderland and explore the beauty it has to offer.

7/9/22
Inspired by snorkelling.

It

Rippling across water, playing over the ground,
Shifting through time, it changes shape and size,
Creeping forward, though it is not alive,
Travelling onwards to match the sun, moon and stars,
Graceful and menacing are but two ways to describe it,
When the hour strikes it will be gone for a while,
Never gone for long, it will slink into view once again.

8/9/22
Inspired by shadows.

The Queen

Very young you were when you ascended to the throne, determined to rule well and make things better,
For many a year you were our Queen, longer than any before you,
Our hearts are saddened that you are no longer with us, but with God your soul now rests,
You ever spent time as you promised you would, bettering our lives and futures,
We loved you so much more than we can express, and this end to your reign will be hard on us all,
You gave us hope and you were always so strong, we will never forget you, our gracious Queen,
Rest in peace our beloved Queen.

9/9/22
Her Royal Highness Queen Elizabeth ll,
21/4/1926 to 8/9/2022.

Nightlight

Glorious is she of the sky, hanging so far above our heads,
The queen of the night, reigning down upon us,
Guiding our steps with her gaze, she loves to look after us,
Her countenance rippling along the surface of the sea, majestic in her pale beauty,
Many praise her gentle glow, wishing they could be as light as she.

9/9/22
Inspired by the moon.

www.ingramcontent.com/pod-product-compliance
Lightning Source LLC
Chambersburg PA
CBHW051717130826
49812CB00034B/1223
* 9 7 8 9 3 9 5 7 8 4 8 8 7 *